Fault Lines

Fault Lines

poems by
Lida Bushloper

Roncador Press

Copyright © 2019, Lida Bushloper
All Rights Reserved

Bushloper, Lida
Fault Lines : poems : Lida Bushloper
2nd ed.
p. cm.
I. American poetry, 21st century.

ISBN (pbk.). 978-0-9600249-0-2
ISBN (e-book). 978-0-9600249-1-9

Cover Design by Karen Bangcot

Roncador Press

To
Rich, Carolyn and Kathie—
without whom, nothing.

Contents

In His Presence 1
Fossil Fuels 2
Public Library, December 24 3
Villanelle 6
Autumn 8
Food Court 9
In Photographs 10
The Way We Live Now 12
Credo 14
Jacaranda 16
Light 17
At the Gym 18
Returning the Purchase 19
I Did a Stupid Thing 21
The Difference 22
The Romance 24
The Good Life 25
Mixed Tape 31
The Halloween Lover 33
Toronto Love Song 34
Stalker 35

Don't Be Too Clean 38
New Dogs in Old Beds 39
Candida's Bed 41
Don't.. 42
Safety Rules 44
Contemplating the Universe... 48
Voyager.. 51
The Morning After.. 52
On Being Invisible 56
The Devil... 57
The Devil His Own Self.. 72
Guilt... 81
Gift Exchange 83
He's a Good Friend of Kissinger's 84
Hurry, Sleep... 88
At Four... 89
South Lawn 90
A Southern Lady 91
The Party 92
Perhaps Someday... 94
To a Survivor 96

After Christmas.. 97
Gone 98
On Her 80th Birthday 99
Belovéd... 100
Shopping 101
In the Throes 102
A Wish List from the Writer 103
Sine Qua Non 104

Acknowledgements 107
About the Author... 109

In His Presence
(for Stephen Hawking)

Slumped low into his chair like rain-soaked cloth,
inert and motionless except for this:
with twitching cheek he speaks through his machine.
By mind alone he holds the gaze of all
who gather here, in unrestricted awe.
Oblivious to hint of drool on lips,
we worship, full of wonder, at his mind,
his vision, reaching past creation's germ,
beyond what we call matter, time or space,
with boldest theories of the universe.
His brain appears to work all on its own.
What needs his body has, we cannot know.
Besides that's not what we revere him for.
The body we respect, of course, for this—
it keeps alive the pulsing intellect.

Fossil Fuels

Gasoline is
fresh cut grass and the
growl of the mower in summer.

Kerosene is
damp tent canvas
and crickets singing.

Motor oil is
sacks of feed, bins of seed and
revving engines at the farm supply store.

Coal tar creosote is
heat rising from the pilings of the dock,
the slap of water, the zing of the fishing line.

Where will memories come from
When fossil fuels are gone from Earth?

Public Library, December 24

Steadily, the rain falls.
Seeping, soaking,
it conquers all—in time.

The ground can hold no more.
The gutters can hold no more.
Creek beds can hold no more.
Catch basins and reservoirs can hold no more.
Still the rain falls.

Sidewalks are sluices.
No place is safe to walk.
Clothes are sodden and heavy.
Trees droop and minds bend
    from the weight of water.
Mold takes hold.

Inside the public library,
    there is warmth and light,
    a few dry chairs.
It is a place to kill time till dinner,
    to escape from loved ones or loneliness.

Volunteers serve hot cider from a steaming urn.

Workers smile and reflect on
    their soon-to-be-reached homes—
    colored lights, cinnamon and pine,
    warm feet in dry slippers.
Even those who live alone find sanctuary
    in their own place.

The dark sky grows darker.
The warning bell rings (it's early closing today).
The patrons—surprising how many there still are—
    pull on damp coats,
    gather belongings,
    check out books,
    struggle to open umbrellas,
    then step out into the wet and the cold,
    first in a trickle, then a flow:

    the elderly couple who must use the bathroom one
        more time before walking the two blocks home,
    the retiree who spends hours tracking his investments,
        dozing over the financial news,
    the composer who covers page after page with notes,
    the magazine browsers,
    the dedicated students,
    the ones who dread going home, but can, and,
    quiet as a drifting mist, barely noticed,
    the man with duct tape binding his canvas shoes.

Villanelle

Flowers and candles on a makeshift shrine
Offer an illusion the community cares.
Maybe, just maybe, it'll work this time.

Every scene of a violent crime
Briefly, magically, fleetingly lures
Flowers and candles for a makeshift shrine.

Drive-by shooting takes a child of nine—
Mother on TV fighting back tears—
Maybe, just maybe that'll work this time.

Shopkeeper picks through the ruins to find
Something to save while the street sweeper clears
Flowers and candles from a makeshift shrine.

Youngest killer makes the cover of *Time*:
Experts, amateurs hustle their cures.
Maybe just one of them'll work this time.

Home invasion is the hot new crime.
Walls and bars push away our fears.
Like flowers and candles on a makeshift shrine.
Who knows, maybe it'll work this time.

Autumn

Autumn means wearing a sweat shirt to bed,
A simmering, peppery stew,
Crackling leaves, sodden leaves, yellow and red,
A cider and cinnamon brew.

Fall is departing geese, honking in flight,
A whispering, foretelling wind,
Curtains drawn sooner, a little each night,
As summer comes to its end.

Food Court

Little boy and little girl
on highest tiptoe, yet
still barely able to see
over the counter's edge
through the Plexiglas
to watch the pretzel maker
roll, flip, twist the dough
then lay it on trays for the oven.
They stretch tall, gape, watch,
until, drawn away by their mother,
they skip and run,
their curiosity intact, enhanced,
eager for the next new thing.

In Photographs

Pretty models learn to pose
With backward glance in ruffled clothes,
Or sitting by a waterfall
Beneath a useless parasol,
Or in a swimsuit all at ease
While grinding sand into their knees.
No matter what discomfort's there
They dare not show a doubt or care.
Their job's to make it credible
For men to think they're beddable,
For men and women both to buy
This carefully constructed lie,
That you can look and live as they—
Just buy this product right away.

An average girl can rest her mind
When caught in photos less than kind.
No image to live up or down,
A slumping shoulder or a frown
Is no deal breaker that's for sure.
We can relax, not just endure.
So whatever joy you see
Or hint of sexuality
Comes from true delight, I'll bet.
What you see is what you get.

The Way We Live Now

When we went on dates
our parents sent us off
with money for cab fare home,
or at least enough
change for a phone call,
along with the
supreme certainty that we had
the option and
the means to leave,
if we needed, or wanted, to.

Later we needed more—
job skills, credit cards,
child care.

Now we need shelters,
restraining orders,
police protection,
notice, care, support

and, crucially,
the self-trust to know
when it's time
(always sooner than later)
to run.

Credo

Whispers, whispers on the air
Speak of things that are not there.
There's no god who justifies
Murder, conquest, sacrifice.

Christian, Muslim, Pagan, Jew—
Any creed can target you.
Jim at Jonestown, Stalin's spree
Differ only in degree.

Planet, species, race, tribe, kin—
No connection saves from sin.
No man's mother is secure
From her son whose aims are pure.

Crystals, channels, mystic chants,
Gurus with their sycophants
Come and go and leave no trace
Of a bettered human race.

Go to Roswell if you must
Seek your truth in desert dust.
Faith in things one cannot see
Kills responsibility.

From this thought most people shrink:
Truth may not be what you think.
Scorn my faith but spare me yours.
Skeptics fight no holy wars.

If we say the truth out loud
We are stoned, or disavowed.
Whispering only do we dare
Speak of things that are not there.

Jacaranda

Mays are not endless.
Neither are Junes,
Nor childhoods, nor lifetimes,
Nor spring afternoons.

So hungrily gaze at
The purple-blue blooms,
That they may live ever
In memory's rooms.

Light

Dawn light expands upward
pushing the darkness out of sight
like yeast expands the dough,
puffing the loaf until the knowing cook
captures it at its peak, for baking.
No skilled baker arrests the day.
The light recedes, the day shrinks
every perfect moment falls,
until the glow of dusk,
dull or brilliant,
painted or grey
tells us that this day, too
has crumbled into night.

At the Gym

I come here faithfully three times a week
to peddle, pump, to lift, to pant and sweat
and just as constantly I dare not speak
the truth: with all this work, no difference—yet.
I follow (mostly) my new eating plan
(a lot of work for hedonistic me),
but still the scale is stuck where I began.
I see no change in shape or energy.
Then why persist without the kind of hope
that keeps one going in the face of lack
of progress? Dread of one more slippery slope.
It only gets much harder to climb back.
I banish wishful thoughts that tempt and lurk.
Fact: idle dreams and short cuts never work.

Returning the Purchase

I need to return this sweater, please.
You'd like to know the reason?
Oh, no, not at all, it fits perfectly.
This designer's line is very flattering,
    and the quality is as good as always.
Well . . . it's just that . . .
I know I'm silly, but . . .
I saw an ad on TV and this lady was
    wearing the same sweater, and hey, it looked
    great on her, too.
But she had Alzheimer's, it was an ad for
    an Alzheimer's drug.
Of course, I know it was really an actress,
    not somebody who actually had Alzheimer's
    but now it creeps me out to wear this sweater.
I'm afraid I'll look like . . .
afraid people will think . . .
    and I'm not,
    not like that character in that ad,
    not sick, or having mental problems . . .
    not old.

Sorry.
Of course, that's more than you needed to know.
Put down whatever reason you want.
It's a lovely sweater but I can't wear it.
I just can't.
Thank you. You've been very kind.

I Did a Stupid Thing

I did a stupid thing (so long ago)
And feel a pang of shame that makes me wince
Each time I hear her name, or his, although
They likely never thought about it since.
I said a cruel thing to someone dear
Who never would have said those words at all
And now I must regret, year after year,
An incident he can't seem to recall.
I cheat and fib and pilfer when I dare,
Then lie awake with fear of getting caught,
When no one seems to notice or to care.
I see a pattern. Here is what I'm taught:
I'm not the focus of the world I'm in—
It's mostly I who suffers from my sin.

The Difference

You're scared.
I can tell.
I know the signs—
the stumbling words
or those withheld,
the actions postponed.

I bear scars, too, like all of us,
from mistakes, betrayal,
rejection, waste.

Perhaps your memory is sharper,
or more recent than mine—
of pain, grief.
Perhaps you suffered more,
or would.

Yes, let's use that to explain
why you hold back, wait for perfect safety
while I, not wiser,
rush headlong to embrace
the imperfect moment.

You, too afraid to act.
Me, too foolish to hold back.

Me, the child who uproots baby carrots,
impatient to see results,
you, who never plants at all.
No harvest for either of us,
just the same.

The Romance

They apologize to each other—
he for failures of attention,
she for unfunny wisecracks.
They want each other's good opinion,
strive to convey caring,
but all efforts fall short,
never really take, progress, gel.
They contemplate each other in confusion,
stuck in the mire of missed signals,
out of sync moods,
misread facial expressions,
moments rushed,
opportunities squandered.
Each wishes for closeness, support, understanding.
Can they ever achieve it?
Sure. Miracles happen every day.

The Good Life

Thank god nobody can hear me think.
I'm not really wishing anybody would die.
It's just that that's the only way I'll ever have anything—
    if somebody dies and leaves me something.
But hell, nobody I know has any money anyway.
I just wish something good would happen, that's all.
Maybe there'll be a disaster.
Okay that's not a good thing, really, but
    then I could be a heroine.
I'd lead everybody on this subway to safety.
My calm strength will reassure them.
They'll turn to me as a natural leader.
I'll make sure the injured aren't left behind to die.
Then I'll be modest and leave the scene.
But the others will marvel about how I saved them all.
Eventually the newspapers will track me down.
Then the talk shows.

The mayor will create a position just for me, like "calmer in chief" or something.
Okay, that's pretty far fetched.
But maybe there'll be something good in the mail when I get home.
Even an ad or a catalog is better than an empty box.
Maybe there'll even be a card.
I can't think of anybody who owes me one, though.
Maybe some friend will call.
She's heard about a great new band playing at a club and wants me to come along.
There was that time I was over at Lucy's returning that book. One of her friends called and asked her to go to a club, so I got asked to go, too. That never happened again, though. I guess Lucy doesn't go out much either.

But this time will be different. We'll meet some guys at the next table.
They'll offer to buy us drinks.
I'll hit it off with the cute one.
Like that guy sitting across from me right now.
What if he gets off at my stop?
What if he stands close behind me on the escalator?
When we get to the street, he'll say,
"You must live around here. Would you like to go for a coffee?"
Then we'd start meeting every day.
Pretty soon he'd confess he loves me desperately.
He'd promise to treat me like a queen, if only I'd marry him.
Maybe I wouldn't really love him as much as he loves me, but I'd marry him because I couldn't bear to break his heart.
He'd do everything for me, I wouldn't have to lift a finger or ever work again.

Oops, there he is, getting off now.
I almost feel like saying, "wait, this isn't our stop!"
I wish something good would happen.
I don't even know what.
But my life is really going nowhere.
At least I have a job. Some people don't even have that much.
Still, I know I could do more.
Being a secretary is okay, but maybe some day, someone will come into the office and see how good I really am.
He'll offer me a job as his personal assistant.
He'll be a rich businessman, and I'll take care of all the details of his life that he can't handle, like his social correspondence, his travel arrangements.
He'll be a widower with two children in boarding school.
On holidays, they will grow very fond of me.

Soon, he'll see that he, too, has grown to love me, and he'll
 ask me to be his wife. Together, we'll help
 struggling artists and support charities. We'll be
 honored by the community for our generous and
 selfless giving.
Well, that's probably not gonna happen.
Maybe I'll just get a raise.
Then I could afford a better apartment, or a trip to Europe.
If I had more money, I could live better.
I bet then exciting things would happen to me.
Here it is, Wednesday night already.
I wish I could think of something fun to do on the weekend.
Well, there's still two days to go.
Maybe I'll come up with something, or maybe somebody
 will call me, or maybe I'll meet someone
 between now and then.

I hate walking home from the subway.
Everybody always hurries away.
They all have somewhere important to go, someone to meet.
I'll bet people call them all the time.
Hey, the newsstand has new issues of my favorite magazines.
May as well buy them all. I'll stop at the store and get some chips and ice cream.
That'll get me through the evening.
And maybe something good will be on TV.
Maybe somebody will call.

Mixed Tape

I track down songs,
borrow from all over,
buy a CD for that one cut
that makes me swoon.

I patiently record
on expensive equipment,
each song that expresses our
mad love, our burning lust
our joy in finding our
one true soul mate.

I make copies for you, for the car, for work—
I listen to it obsessively.

Then the unexpected, yet expected, breakup comes,
when I see you for who you really are,
not Prince Charming after all,
not the soul mate I thought you were,
and see myself—let's face it, no princess either.
Now the tape,
which captured the greatest love ever known
between two people,
lies in a sack of discards
in the garage,
gathering dust.

The Halloween Lover

My lover came to visit Halloween,
his face made up so very like a ghoul,
I shrank in startled fear, then felt a fool,
for thinking him a stranger never seen.
Yet all the evening I was filled with dread.
I told myself, it's still his hands, his eyes.
His eerie silence, part of his disguise,
enhanced the wrongful image in my head.
He'll wash it off tomorrow or tonight,
but still for me that image will remain.
And what if it had been a lasting stain?
Is my affection solely based on sight?
I'll never see him like I did before.
I'd loved more for the surface than the core.

Toronto Love Song
(for R.W.)

When you lay down this night, this night,
did you think of me here in the city?
For I did sorely long for you
as tiredness kissed and caressed me.

No more will I know your warm bigness,
nor stiff, sweet brush of your beard.
For we are apart now forever,
each on our own chosen road.

Stalker

My stalker is dead.
All threats are off. You'd think.
I've lived with this shadowy menace for so long,
had to be steadfast, on guard, for so long,
the fear does not evaporate but
lingers like the imprint of a heavy load on one's shoulders
or a bad odor in the house or on one's clothes.
I open the windows, scrub clothes on rocks,
but it takes time.

Years ago I shed everything he had touched,
shredded pictures,
purged the house and car,
even gave away the diamond necklace
he once pressed on me.
To wear it, even without his knowing,
would seem somehow to encourage him,
to express acceptance.
That he lived 3000 miles away was little comfort,
not with air travel, the Internet
and my own damnable good memory.

We cling to treasured memories, knowing with grief
that no matter how hard we try to hang on,
they will fade and wink out.
Bad memories cling to us, their only source of life.

I tell myself I no longer need to fear a ringing phone,
a doorbell chime,
or him Googling my name, fishing for news.
I can stop flinching when I open the mail box, email,
or my bank statement.

I no longer need to apologize to family, friends, colleagues,
innocents whose only fault is their attachment to me,
for his unwanted attentions,
all the while knowing, *knowing*, he was winning,
as he repeatedly forced himself upon my thoughts.

Every change—welcome or not—takes getting used to,
time to sink in, meld into the background of life.
Castaneda was right about fear—
it goes away gradually, *and* it goes away all at once.
When the phone rings, I still fear it's him,
his ghost.
But experience has given me faith.
At some future moment, I'll be going about my day,
showering or tidying or walking,
when suddenly it'll hit me—
I'm not thinking about him—and can't remember the last time I did.

Don't Be Too Clean

Don't be too clean. Just let your hygiene lapse
enough to bring your essence to the fore.
I need to know I've filled in all the gaps
of who you are before I can be sure.
Don't leave it up to me to guess the facts
or flaws that you've, with perfect guile, disguised,
to then recoil from unexpected acts
and hear you say, "You should have realized . . ."
You cannot every moment be on guard.
You think you're fooling people. You can't hide
forever what you are. It's much too hard
to bury human weakness deep inside.
I have a right to know your greatest sin.
Don't be too clean—if only now and then.

New Dogs in Old Beds

When the last of the old dogs died and
could no longer be upset by newcomers,
J and K adopted 2 new puppies and
commenced fighting over every little thing.
He resented the attention she paid to them,
which he thought should be his, now that the previous dogs,
sick, lame, needy in their old age, were finally gone.
She bristled at what, to her, was his
cavalier treatment of them when
she was sure they needed constant care,
assiduous, meticulous.
Both remained persistently oblivious that there
was more behind it.
The new family called it all up—
30 years of truncated griefs, unmet needs, nagging guilt,
lingering mistrust, unreciprocated concessions,
disappointed hopes—

which they believed had been dealt with,
buried, and paved over,
but lay there still,
contaminating the soil,
like a toxic waste dumping ground
kept secret by a corrupt government.
The pups, boisterous in play,
replete with cuddling,
thrived.

Candida's Bed

When Candida remained with
" . . . the weaker of the two."
She knew what she was in for.
Do you?

There is no gratitude.
They take it as their due.
I didn't know that then.
Do you?

Was Candida a martyr?
Was she hard done by,
Or just a foolish altruist?
Was I?

If given a second chance
After time went by,
Would she choose the same?
Will I?

Don't

Don't cut down the trees
for me.
Yes, they obscure the moon.
Yes, I told you I love to gaze at it,
when it's full, or surrounded by
a ring of crystals, or
low and orange in autumn, or
as it illuminates the wet summer pasture.
But the moon will rise over the tallest tree tops
in time. I can wait,
and while I wait
I love just as much
the mosaic of silver shards gleaming
through the tangle of black branches,
the pied precursor
to the imperfect pearl,
whose craters and peaks
make me love it more.

The trees do not block my view, but
whet my desire for what's to come,
like a warm-up act before
the star performer takes the stage.
You say you love me and want to fulfill
my every wish.
Don't cut down the trees,
for me.

Safety Rules

Don't smile at that man.
It's too dangerous.
He might come over and talk to us.
He might make you laugh.
He might like you, spend time with you,
    a lot of time, time enough to get to know you and
    find out what you're really like.
But by then you'll have fallen in love with him
    so that when he finds out how you really are and
    breaks it off
    you'll get your heart broken.
And nobody knows who he is.
Who are his people?
Does he come from a good family?
Is he well-off?
You're a little gullible.
You could get taken in by some fast talker
    who thinks *you* have money.
You can't be too careful.

Don't take that trip.
It's much too far.
Isn't that a dangerous area right now?
If you fall or get sick, how will you get home?
It's too expensive anyway.
You need to save your money.
You might need it later.
Maybe even for a wedding.
And why do you want to spend two weeks
    with a bunch of strangers?
It'll just be money wasted.
Remember, men don't like women who are too independent.
You could spend your vacation here and we can do things
    together.

Don't apply for that promotion.
It you don't get it, you'll know it means
    you're not good enough and just end up feeling
    worse about yourself.
You'll give your boss the wrong idea.

He'll think you're unhappy.
You have to show some loyalty, or act like you do.
He'll find some excuse to get rid of you.
No. It's better to stay where you are, not risk a chance.
It doesn't cost anything to stay where you are.
Take time to think about it.
Another chance will come along some time.
Besides, men don't like women who make a lot of money.

I wouldn't take that class if I were you.
You'll never be good at that and
    all the other students will be younger than you
    and they'll just laugh at you for even trying.
You certainly won't meet any men your age there.
You won't do very well anyway and
then you'll be sorry you wasted all that time,
    not to mention money.

It's too hard.
It's too tedious.
And if you fail it'll depress you.
It'll just make you feel like you can't do anything.
But I know you can.
There's plenty to learn without going to a class.
Why don't you ask me? I can teach you stuff—
    all about entertaining and table setting.
Stuff you'll need to know when you marry the right man,
    a man who's going places in this world.
What? Of *course* you'll marry.
I'm hurt to hear you say that.
Why, any man in this world would be lucky, lucky to get
    you for a wife.
You're beautiful, charming, smart.
You'll find someone who can see all your good qualities
    and all you have to offer.
If anything, none of them are good enough for *you*.
No, I *know*, *my* girl will marry and marry well.
It's what I brought you up for.
And until then you have a wonderful life,
    happy and safe, right here.

Contemplating the Universe

Saw Stephen Hawking on TV last night.
Let's see if I can get this right—
    something about the positive energy
    and the negative energy being equal
    so it's always a net zero
Hey, Netzero, remember them?
Wonder if they're still around.
Well, that's not important.
What I mean is, we've always known that that particular
    natural law was true about fat, that there's never a net
    loss of fat in the world,
        that when one person takes it off, it doesn't die or
        disappear, it just migrates to someone else,
        someone else's hips or thighs or whatever.
So we look with dread at anyone who's dropping a few
    pounds,
        and even while we're glad for them, if it's one of our
        friends, we silently plead, "not me, not me,"

    then feel crappy for wishing it on someone else,
    like that guy in *1984*—
    "Julia, do it to Julia."
So yeah, we know it works for fat.
The only thing science doesn't know yet, is whether the fat can
    travel world-wide, or does it have to attach itself to someone nearby, like in it's own
    galaxy.
But what I really wonder, 'cause I've observed this,
    is whether it's true for relationships.
See, it just seems like when one couple is breaking up
    somebody else is getting together.
Like there has to be a fixed number of couples in the universe,
    no net gain or loss.

So, if you see two people getting together, you start to look at your
partner differently,
with a little fear and suspicion and already a twinge of grief, and
you say the same mantra, "not us, please, not us."
But it has to work the other way, too.
So, can it possibly mean, since my friends Charlotte and Will are splitting up
(which I DO NOT wish for, I don't wish that for anyone)
that I might be hooking up with some new love, myself, maybe soon?

Voyager

I followed you beneath the earth
Then into outer space.
And as we sank I lost my heart—
Your mind its resting place.

And as we fell and rose again
In rhythmic harmony,
A light ignited in my soul
To burn eternally.

The Morning After

Crap. Damn it. I'm such an idiot.
What is wrong with me?
I screwed up again.
Why did I act like that?
I did it all wrong.
I blew it.
I should have let him talk more.
I shouldn't have smiled so much.
It looks desperate.
I shouldn't have tried to be funny.
That really fell flat.
I shouldn't have spilled my guts.
TMI, TMI.
Why can't I learn to hold back?
Why can't I learn to be cool?
But no, I just blather on.
He was nice enough not to be rude, but it was
    pretty obvious he was getting turned off.

Like when he tried to start up conversations with some
    of the other people around.
But that fell flat, too, no fault of mine.
Well, to give myself some credit, I did try to ask him stuff.
But what can you do when all you get is one-word answers.
And when he does talk, he won't look at you.
You can see his eyes dart around the room.
Well, screw him.
He probably wasn't worth it anyway.
I noticed he wasn't exactly surrounded by adoring women.
And what's wrong with him?
How come he doesn't know how to gracefully
    exit himself from the situation, instead of hanging
    around me all night?
Hell, even I know how to do that.
Had to do it plenty of times.

Like when that one guy from Paraguay or wherever glommed
 onto me at that conference last month.
Talk about a fish out of water.
It didn't take long before I could see why he was desperate for company.
BORing.
Besides I could barely understand a word he said.
Yeah he spoke English but it was with a pretty thick accent.
Luckily, somebody from another group called me over and I never went back in his direction.
Well, I hope I didn't hurt his feelings.
I never want to do that.
I felt a little sorry for him.
It can't be easy, being dropped down in the middle of a foreign country to do a job, no friends, no family, strange food and all.

But hey, I'm just making all that up.
How do I know he doesn't have friends?
Maybe, I hope, he found someone else that he could
   hang out with,
     someone who enjoyed talking to him.
And I wasn't hurt last night, myself.
Not really.
Can't blame a guy for being put off when
   I acted like that.
Stupid, stupid, stupid.
I certainly humiliated myself.
It makes me never, ever want to leave the house again.
When will I ever learn?
Well, I'd better get on up.
Don't want to be late for work.

On Being Invisible

There are those times we wish that we could be
like Harry Potter, with a magic cloak
that gives a safe invisibility,
concealing us from other threatening folk.
We slip into a doorway when we spy
a jilted lover we're ashamed to face.
We carefully avoid the boss's eye
when "volunteers" are needed anyplace.
We hope, if ever in an angry mob,
not being seen will save us from attacks.
But wait awhile. Old age will do the job,
as youth and beauty's mostly what attracts.
I pick the fruit from strangers' laden trees,
escaping notice with disturbing ease.

The Devil

An old man is the Devil.
He drives oh so carefully,
he slows down when he gets anywhere near the intersection
instead of speeding up like normal people in order to
    make the light.
What does he care if he misses the green light and
has to wait for the lights to cycle all the way through
yellow and red and then to green again
which means of course that everyone behind him has
    to wait.
He stops on yellow, or in anticipation of yellow,
he follows all the traffic laws,
he stops for pedestrians even if
they are miles from the corner and sauntering
so he'd have plenty of time to turn right or scoot
through the intersection and besides
they may not even want to cross the street,
how can you even tell from such a distance away?

God forbid him to ever be in a hurry.
He doesn't care if other people are late for
work—through no fault of their own—late
for the third time this month,
late because your husband won't lift a finger to help
and you've got kids to feed, plus the dog and
you were up late arguing
about the same crap over and over
and just couldn't get up on time
and you're terrified you might be pregnant again
and you hate the job and the boss but you need
every penny because your husband doesn't make much either
and besides what other jobs are out there and
the whole time you're driving to work you know
you're almost out of gas, but you can't take time to
fill up because you're already late, but if you run out
of gas you'll really be late then and you will NOT think

about the brake light that stays lit or calculate the last
time you got new tires because repairs are out of the question
right now, but you've got to keep this car going, you'd
    never be able
to leave the house in time to get the bus and you can't get a
job closer to home, there's just nothing out there, and
besides, I'm not fit for anything else,
he keeps insisting,
he tells me all the time how dumb I am, so somehow I
have to hang on to the job I have I can't be late again
but maybe this time nobody will notice, but somehow they
always know, but hell, everybody else gets away with it
why is it always me who has to bump into the boss just as
I'm running in the door, other people seem to hurry in when
he's got his back turned and nobody would ever snitch,
they all stick together but everybody else gets away
    with it,
while I get the funny, sarcastic, skeptical looks—
hell

I wish he would just go ahead and get that damn time clock
he's always threatening to get,
then all those cheaters would finally get caught, but right now
it seems like it's always just me. And then I either have to get
my pay docked for the fifteen minutes or stay late to make
    it up
and I don't dare do that, ever, ever, 'cause
I get nothing but complaints and questions about it at
    home and suspicion.
There the light's finally green, but he barely can get
his creaky old foot on the accelerator and get that heap
    moving.
An old man is the Devil.

An old man is the Devil.
He creeps along in the grocery store,
his cart parked exactly in the middle
of the aisle, it doesn't occur to him

to leave room for anybody else
while he studies the ingredients on a can of corn
(oh for god's sake, it's CORN)
as if at his age it really matters any more
what crap he eats or doesn't eat,
oblivious to others who might be in a hurry
to get home to cook and clean
and who have a crying child and another one whining
for toys and candy that you
can't afford and besides if you give in,
it'll only be worse next time and
you're trying to juggle coupons and keep a tally in your head
because you only have so much to spend
and now he holds the can a bit away from his face and
tilts his head back to peer through the lower part of his
bifocals and angles the can to catch the light because
the print really is too small
(I'll give him that, half the time I can't make it out myself

but who can afford glasses besides I'm too young)
but he reads it, out of curiosity or because he watches
    TV all day long and
keeps hearing about all the bad things in food,
the same food he's eaten all his life,
or his wife or his doctor told him something to watch out for
or hell, he's just got time on his hands,
why not, no hurry, not all that much to do at home.
An old man is the Devil when he jokes with the young
(or not so young, but plenty younger than he is)
cashier and she's just trying to move the line along but
    he tells her
80-year-old jokes until finally he gets the nerve to tell the
one he considers dirty because somewhere it has the word
    "bra" in it
and tells it clumsily and it's old and stupid and not funny,
but he thinks he's saucy to tell it and he thinks he's flirting
and because she giggles politely,
he's reassured himself that he's still attractive

to every woman on the face of the earth,
quite the rake, the man about town, the roué, a charmer,
   a wit, a card, sweet, cute,
he calls her "honey" and says "Smile, you look prettier
   that way,"
things he would never say to a woman his own age,
or to a man, and he misses entirely her
discomfort, contempt, perhaps even anger
because in customer service you mask what you feel and
   besides,
she just needs to get him to move on,
the line behind him is growing and
they're short staffed today
and because she's young and needs the job and she's well
   trained,
she endures things she'd never put up with out on the
   street and
that he wouldn't dare say to anyone who's not a captive
   audience

and because they're short staffed there's only one line and
time is ticking on and you're starting to get desperate because
you know you HAVE to be back at the exact time you
    said you would
because if you aren't there'll be hell to pay and
the questions and accusations and suspicions will start and
nothing you answer will be believed or be good enough
and especially if you bought even one thing not on the list,
just because you didn't remember till you got there
that you were out of something,
then he accuses you of lying and then of flirting and
then of meeting someone secretly and
nothing you do stops him from believing it and
even if he hasn't been drinking it will be hell and
you don't know how bad it'll get
or how long it will go on this time,
or how it will end up, but by god

it's been getting worse it seems like and
comes more often and with less to set it off
so for god's sake you HAVE to get out of this line,
out of this store, get home, break laws, run lights if you
 have to,
but get home on time, but sometimes even that doesn't work,
he finds something else, he always finds something,
but what can I do, with the kids and all, where can I go,
he'd find me and then it would be worse than ever.
I can't just abandon the cart
I have to go home with the groceries,
proof that I was where I said I was going, and
he won't ever come with me, it's like he sets me up.
I wish I hadn't let him make me quit my job, but
he just kept nagging and nagging and
telling me how much he wanted me at home, spending
all my time taking care of him and
the kids and how he made plenty of money
but now I have no one but him to talk to or depend on and
please for god's sake SHUT UP and MOVE you old fart,

I'd like to ram my cart into his old, wrinkled, bony butt—
there he finally takes his receipt and moves, and
don't you DARE think of one more thing to ask or tell,
    no, he's leaving.
An old man is the devil.

An old man is the Devil
with time on his hands, he's retired,
he was a lawyer, a professor, owned a business,
whatever, but basically a windbag and
now nobody listens to him because they don't have to
    anymore,
he's not the boss but he needs his fix, still needs an
    audience and
his wife at home isn't gonna put up with it, she
see's right through him, doesn't, never did, think
he was the king of the world, plus,
she's finally gotten him out of the house
for an hour or two

so here he stands in front of the librarian
with his jokes and his pointless questions,
you bet he's not about to learn how to use the computer,
lord no, that would mean he'd have to do it himself and
not have someone's full attention on him while he
refuses to get to the point, no matter how skillful the
    librarian is,
and she's pretty damn good,
but he still insists on telling her WHY he needs to know
which order the stripes are on the Irish flag and
which order the same color stripes are on the Ivory Coast
    flag because
he's sure the radio guy got it wrong and
he wants to call in and set him straight and maybe win
    a tee shirt,
or else he needs the address of an army general
whose picture he saw in the paper,
the name is so similar to someone he met at a party years ago,
it might be the same guy and wouldn't that be interesting, and

he knows so many important people,
or he wants to win a bet with the fellows he meets for coffee
every morning at MacDonald's and
so he needs to know exactly WHEN the New Orleans Jazz became the Utah Jazz,
he'll show those bozos that he knows what he's talking about and
he's oblivious to the line growing behind him and
the librarian nodding at the others to let them know
she'll get with them as soon as she can and
he's going deaf but is too stubborn to admit it,
which forces the librarian to nearly shout,
disturbing everyone else around, but he doesn't care
as long as he gets the information and really, the attention, he wants,
he's doesn't care that other people have a class to get to in 10 minutes,

other people who couldn't get to the library earlier because
they work two jobs and juggle child care and
are putting themselves through school and
by the time they got here all the computers were occupied
    and
who forgot to write down just one citation and
whose paper is due tomorrow and
whose class doesn't get out till 10:00 PM
when the library will be closed and
who has to get to work early to print out her paper because
her old printer died and she can't afford a new one or to
    get hers fixed and
if I can just get through this semester
maybe during the break I can scrounge around and find
    one and
I can't get to the computer lab at school because I work
    two jobs

to support the kids and I HAVE to succeed,
have to make good grades, I need the financial aid,
'cause I can barely make it as it is and
now that I've finally, somehow,
gotten away, I'm terrified that if I fail I'll have to go back or
he'll get the kids and then he'll have all that power over me again
and why can't that old fucker come to the library when it's not busy,
what's wrong with him that he can't show any consideration
for anyone else or for god's sake don't they have ANYone else
who can step in and help, we all need help, it's not just me
and besides, damn it, this is a college library,
why can't he go and bother them at the public library?
I'll tell you why, it's because coming to the college
makes him think he's superior somehow,
like he's smarter or too good for the mere public library with its

hoi polloi, that if he gets his info here it's got more quality, what a jackass,
at least if I'm late to class I can't get fired for it,
I'm just so afraid I might miss something and all because of this asshole with his pretensions and selfishness—
thank god the librarian finally invoked the "rule" (if there really is one, ha ha,)
only two reference questions at a time and
then she has to help the next person and
he has to get back at the end of the line, if he needs more help and
he's surprised, so surprised, when he finally turns around and
notices the line behind him and
gives an apologetic smile, but what the fuck good does that do now—
he is an old man,
he is the Devil.

The Devil His Own Self

I used to be such a devil.
I could dance all night with a dozen different girls.
Heck, I didn't have to ask them.
They'd ask me.
Helps to be a good dancer.
Maybe I was just willing.
Maybe I was more willing than good.
But I sure enjoyed myself.
Now? Dance? Heck, I can barely walk.
But I'm doing better now, I think.
Now that they took the car away, I'm walking more.
They said I couldn't see.
Got pulled over by a cop.
He said I ran a stop sign and I made the mistake of saying
    I hadn't seen it.
Thank god it was somebody I knew, a boy who used to
    be in Scouts with my boy,
      otherwise he might have run me in.

(Boy? Heck, my son's 52 this year. I don't like to think about it, though.

Makes me feel old.)

Instead he just called my daughter and made me give her my keys.

I don't suppose I'll ever get 'em back, now.

That dancing with all the girls, though, my wife put an end to that.

We'd still go out, after we married, and I was still dancing with everybody.

I didn't see why things should be any different.

I was just trying to be nice, not let girls sit there all night.

But she said I couldn't act that way any more.

It rankled a bit, but I got used to it and settled down.

The girls sure hated that.

Now I'd give my right arm if I could just hear my wife fuss at me one more time about
    something . . .

I used to laugh at her sometimes, that just made her more mad.
But we always made it up in the end.
Anyway, I'm lucky about where I live.
I can walk to the senior center for bingo, walk to the dry cleaners and the coffee shop.
There's a little grocery store not too far away.
I like to go in there and tease the girls.
I know some of 'em don't like it, and I try to stay away from them.
Hey, I'm old, not stupid.
But some of the others, heck, it cheers 'em up.
I like going to the store, but it's hard, too.
I know I don't eat very well, not like I should.
I try to eat like my wife would want me to.
She always made sure I ate right, said she wanted to have me around for a long time—
and then look what happened.
She went first.

But I'm trying to be careful about what I eat—read labels and all.
In fact, I try to do everything the way she would have wanted.
I tried to make her happy for nearly 60 years. I guess I hope somehow she sees it and
 knows I still love her.
And about the car, maybe it was about time.
I know people got irritated at me.
Sometimes they'd even honk their horns.
Screw them, wait till they get my age and it hurts to move their neck around to see over
 their shoulder and they can't quite see out of the corners of their eyes anymore.
Wait till they've had a couple of bad accidents, maybe even hurt somebody, then they'll
 start being more careful.
Then someday they'll have to give it up altogether, just like I did.

And they'll hang on as long as they can, too, just like I
 did.
When I was just out of the Navy, I saved up and bought
 a little yellow sports car.
I think my wife fell in love with that car as much as she
 did with me.
I sure as hell did.
But I wrecked it and I knew then that it was too much
 temptation—you know, speeding,
 dashing in and out of traffic, beating everybody else
 away from the light—I admit I
 was showing off.
I knew it would be too easy to wreck the next one.
Besides, we had a little one on the way by then.
So, the next car was a sedan.
Never went back to the sports cars after that.
Guess I grew up a little.
Most people do.

And the ones that don't, well they cause most of the trouble in the world, my opinion
anyway.
I hate not being able to drive to the college, though, and use their library.
I liked being around all the young students.
They're so alive, so carefree.
And I was just getting ready to start taking computer classes at the public library.
But it's too far to walk, and the Dial-a-Ride, well, you just can't depend on it.
I do regret that.
I really wanted to learn about computers, see what the fuss was all about.
Plenty guys my age are doing it, emailing their grandkids and all.
Besides, I love learning new stuff. When I was 60 I went back to the college and got my B.A. Not that I really did anything with it, but lord, my wife and kids were so proud of me.

I hate to think those days are over.
If I could learn computers, I could take one of those "on
　　line" classes everybody's talking
　　about.
But I don't see any way I can do that, now, do you?
The senior center, they have classes, but who the heck
　　wants to learn how to silk screen a
　　scarf?
So now I just walk.
At least it's safe.
And I am doing better, I swear.
Except—
　　the other day on the way home from the store I didn't
　　feel so good.
And it scared me a little.
I stopped to rest on a park bench.
One of the gals from the store came along, walking home
　　I guess, and stopped to ask me
　　if I was all right.

That scared me even more.
My lord, did I look that bad?
I guess to her I must have.
It stung a little, having her treat me like somebody sick
	or old.
But at the same time, it made this old heart feel good, to
	know somebody cared a little.
I told her I was fine, I was just starting to walk more and
	it was harder than I thought it
	would be.
She said, don't worry, you'll get stronger, you'll get better.
Thank god she was mostly a stranger.
With your kids you always have to put a good face on
	things, otherwise, they're out
	pricing assisted living apartments.
You should put on a good face for strangers, too, after all,
	you can't burden them with
	your troubles.

They got troubles of their own.
But sometimes when it's a stranger, you let your guard down.
Or maybe it was just that, for one moment, whether it was
    genuine or not, somebody was
    acting like they cared.
Or maybe I was more scared than I knew.
But whatever it was, I broke down. I couldn't help myself.
I blurted it out.
"No, I don't think I will.
I don't think I'll be getting better."
She patted my shoulder.
She wasn't going to accept that.
So for her, I put my game face back on.
But in that instant, my heart had told me the truth.
Sometimes, like it or not, you know.
You know.
You just know.

Guilt

I never got the point about guilt.
I've had Catholic friends with Catholic guilt,
Jewish friends with Jewish guilt, and
believe me, there's plenty of Protestant guilt to be dealt out,
    which is what I was supposed to have.
It was reinforced (no, it wasn't) working in Catholic-run
    hospitals, with Catholic-raised women,
    who muttered, not really to themselves,
    about the virtues of constant cleaning, dusting,
    keeping busy, being useful, putting others first—
    not so different from my bordering-on-fundamentalist
    Protestant mother, who,
    with her extreme prejudices, would have been
    surprised and a little vexed, to find
    she agreed with any Catholic, about anything,
    anything at all.

The Protestant guilt centered
   seriously on matters of sexuality.
The terrors and dread consequences of loose behavior were
   thumped into my mind in the shrillest possible terms.
None of it took.
I am sometimes idle,
   selfish,
   blithe about dust,
   unchaste in thought and deed, and
   cheerful pretty much all the time.

Gift Exchange

My best friend joined a ladies' choir. I'm stuck
Attending each performance, spring and fall.
When she bemoans the time required and all,
I hope she'll soon be quitting—no such luck.
Don't get me wrong, the programs are first-rate,
Especially since they're amateurs, not pros.
They never seem to notice when I doze.
I certainly would never drag a date.
The party afterwards is not so bad.
(Small talk with strangers—always so much fun.)
The church hall's cold. At least we're nearly done.
My dressy clothes are itching just a tad.
Then I remember what she is to me—
A cheering section for my poetry.

He's a Good Friend of Kissinger's

Eddie. Wow, you're home.
Usually I just get your machine.
Yeah, it's Paul, why are you so surprised?
Oh, that, yeah, I'm using my sister's phone.
Doing great, yeah, listen.
You know a lot of people.
I need to find some work, just for, maybe 4 or 5 weeks.
I just need enough to fly down to Rio.
Oh, I don't know, management's what I'm best at,
    but I'll look at other options.
Just don't let anybody know I'm not gonna be there long.
Yeah, I met this guy from Bolivia and he said all the good
    computer people, as soon as they can get out,
    they all fly up here to get good jobs.
So what I figure, all I have to do to make a lot of money
    is get down there—

What? La Paz? It is?
Oh, well, wherever, and set up a school for computer technicians
 and they'll be beating down the door.
I figure I can make enough in a year to be able to finish school.
Nah, language is no problem.
You know, you just learn the basic verb forms, the irregular verbs,
 the rest is just vocabulary.
I can pick it up in a few weeks, while I'm getting the money together to get down there.
Nah, they're not picky about licenses and stuff.
I can figure all that out later.
Yeah, I'm still in pre-archeological studies
 but lately I've gotten hooked on futurism, you know,
I think that may be where it's really at today, taking the future and molding it the way
 it oughta be.

It may be where I can really use my talents to benefit the world,
    plus it includes all my interests, economics, science, the works,
    so I don't have to stick to one thing.
No, that's all taken care of for now, yeah, I moved back in with my parents, just until I leave for Rio.
Okay, La Paz.
Anyway, I had this dynamite weekend, you wouldn't believe.
I spent the whole weekend at this guy's house, some guy I met
    through my sister and there was this other guy there, he's like a composer, I mean he's
    done everything, educational TV, commercials, you name it, and he's so good, he
    made a million dollars by the time he was 22 years old, but he blew it all in one year,
    just on drugs, private jets to Hawaii, cars,
    like he thought he was so rich he could have anything.

Anyway he's just started to get back on his feet, all the time people
 are calling him for songs and trying to get him for this show or the other.
So, this guy has this friend who's an Olympic champion from
 Germany and he was showing us slides on his computer of
 some people and all of a sudden there's this Olympic champ in Mexico City with his
 arm around Henry Kissinger.
It turns out this guy was a really good friend of Kissinger's before he died.
What? He is? Oh. Well I guess I'll get to meet him myself after all.
It just goes to show, you never know who you're gonna meet in this world.
Connections are everything, right?
Oh, sorry, I should have asked if you were in the middle of something. Well, I'll let you go then.
But don't forget, if you hear about any good jobs,
 let me know, will ya?

Hurry, Sleep

Too tired tonight to do another thing,
too tired to love or read another word,
yet burning up to grasp as much of life
as possible for any human soul,
I long for quick oblivion to come
to banish swarming, roiling thoughts that try
to live the coming day before it's born—
a useless exercise that only keeps
the mind imprisoned in its wakeful state.
The sooner I can sleep, the sooner wake,
refreshed and strong with every sense restored,
to rush, reach out for each experience
that comes my way, each thrill or joy or ache,
rejoicing even in the dread or hurt
that lets me know I go on living still.
Please hurry, Sleep. Don't make me wait tonight.

At Four

I sat beside my mother
at the Formica table
in the scrubbed, sunlit kitchen.
The still, quiet morning surrounded us.
I watched idly as she took
objects from a dusty cardboard box,
laid them side by side on the table.
I didn't know what the writing said on
the yellowing white envelopes, or
on the cards that she took out and read to herself.
I didn't know whose lock of hair that was.
I didn't know what the little string of beads was,
nor the swatch of pink cotton or length of lace.
I didn't know why my mother turned her face
away from me, towards the window, silent.
I was shocked when I glimpsed the tears,
shocked to learn that mamas could cry.

South Lawn

Two little girls roll down the grassy slope,
both dressed in denim shorts, their hair in braids.
They giggle, fall, get scraped, they punch and kick
each other. When their mother wants to take
a snap, they strike a body builder's pose.

She never says to them in warning tones,
"Act like a lady. Girls are not supposed
to be like boys are, strong and tough and free."—
a phrase once said—so long ago—to me.

A Southern Lady

Born on a farm, she barely went to school
and hid her lack of training all her life.
Her greatest fear was looking like a fool.
She studied hard to be a fitting wife.
She lived by rules she hoped would keep her safe.
Her Bible and her book of etiquette
were equal guides, though they were known to chafe
her children (who acknowledge now their debt).
Her worthlessness was all inside her head.
She fought self-doubt by gleaning, if she could,
what richer people wore or ate or said,
what was expected, proper, right or good.
She never saw how she was glorified—
still craving reassurance when she died.

The Party

They chat in French, they sip Cointreau
they praise the new bassoonist from Madrid,
and all the while I sit and dare not show
the gulf between their lives and mine, kept hidden by my smile. I know I don't fit in.

On visits home I listen to the talk:
how many billies born, how many nannies,
the new preacher, will she work out,
a great cake recipe— "I really shouldn't."
They ask about my life and once again
I hide behind my smile. I don't fit in.

I ride the rocky platform in between
the world of family, the best of souls,
schoolmates loved but left behind,
every heart never less than kind,

still glad to see me even as I am,
and that other sphere I never can attain,
though they are kind as well, without fail.

Convinced that I'm a misfit everywhere,
I call no place my home—not here, not there.

Perhaps Someday

Perhaps someday I'll give in.
I'll stop insisting I'm fine.
It's not that bad.
No need to worry.

I'm the cowboy with the bullet
wound who says, "Aw, it's just
a scratch."

Perhaps someday
they'll stop saying
"cheer up,'
"look at this gorgeous morning," and
finally,
"what's the matter with you?"

Perhaps someday I'll give up feeling
weak, foolish, immoral, fearful
lazy, silly, petty, proud, vain
and burdensome.

But not yet. For now, I'm still convinced
I can somehow stave off winter, win the
footrace against the tidal wave
and rise out of the inhaling chasm
with a simple change of mind.

To a Survivor

Ever after
you'll wake at that hour
feel your heart pound
listen hard for that sound
praying it's not what you hear—

waiting in terror
for seconds to pass
and hoping to sleep
at dawn.

After Christmas

My sister came to take me to the plane.
She brought her husband, too; he would remain
To help my parents pack their lights and tree,
Distracting them from thoughts of missing me.

But what is there to help control *my* tears
(An ache I never felt till recent years)
At seeing them so frail, not knowing when,
Or even if, I would see them again?

There was a time when I was glad to go,
Could only see such faults as we all show.
But now I know each time may be our last,
I only see their love—so fierce, so vast.

Gone

If we had gone to visit Norma
I planned to take the uke.
She loved to sing and play—
it reminded her of her parents.
She told me her favorites,
Side by Side and *Tumbling Tumbleweeds*—
but we never did go, did we?
Here the uke sits.

On Her 80th Birthday

It's been a while since, with my sister, I
have bought my mother anything. We mean
to show our love, so we decline to buy
another trinket she must dust or clean.
Instead we try methodically to think
of gifts that ease her life or soothe her mind.
We take her out to tea, unclog her sink
and hide distressing news of any kind.
Yet, even now, she mostly yearns to feed
her children and against all pain defend
us, which is just what we no longer need.
We do not lie—but sometimes we pretend.
I let her serve me vegetables and meat
that she has cooked. I let her watch me eat.

Belovéd

Once, you
sprinted up rock-strewn trails,
darted across tennis courts,
jitterbugged and tangoed,
walked the gunnels of bobbing boats
stern to bow.

Now you shuffle, hesitate.
Sidewalk cracks, buckled linoleum,
a throw rug by the door
have become hazards, risks,
the lodestone of your attention,
you, who never noticed them before—
and never dreamed you would.

Shopping

I think today
I'll buy a pie
just in case
the kids come by
and bring their kids.
That way I'll have
something fun
for them to try.

I think I'll buy
a frozen pie
just in case
they don't come by

today.

In the Throes

I turn out the light
I can't sleep
I hear the clock tick
I can't sleep
I throw back the blanket
I throw back the sheet
I can't sleep
I can't sleep
I can't sleep

A Wish List from the Writer

Just one Sarah Brightman note,
Just one *Starry Night*,
A mere *Adagio for Strings*,
A Margot Fonteyn flight.

I can't compose or paint.
My voice won't break a heart.
With words alone I strive
To manifest my art.

Sine Qua Non

If you want to write
I'll tell you what you need:
clean hair,
clean clothes,
a made bed,
cooked meals waiting
in fridge or freezer,
bills paid,
animals petted,
walked,
groomed,
emails answered,
trash taken out,
library books
read and returned,
exercise taken,
birthday cards sent,
car washed and

gassed up,
prescriptions filled,
laundry folded,
appointments made,
dishes washed,
teeth brushed,
weeds pulled,
shopping done,
web surfed,
games played,
death delayed.

Acknowledgements

"Gift Exchange" is reprinted from *The Lyric*.
"On Her 80th Birthday" is reprinted from *The Formalist*.
"Perhaps Someday . . ." is reprinted from *1000 Views of Girl Singing*, John Bloomberg-Rissman, ed.
"Wish List from a Writer" is reprinted from *Writer's Journal*.
"Autumn" appeared, in a slightly different form, in *The Lyric*.

About the Author

Lida Bushloper is an eclectic writer and poet. Her work has appeared in *The Lyric*, *The Formalist*, *Grit*, *Better Homes and Gardens*, *The Huntington Library Quarterly*, *The Explicator* and many confession magazines. Her short mystery fiction has appeared in *Mysterical-e*, *Kings River Life* and *Flash Bang Mysteries*. Her story, "The Wannabe," is included in the anthology *Fishy Business*, published by Wildside Press. Her essay, "My World Champion Sister," was included in *In Celebration of Sisters*, edited by Trisha Faye. She was the winner of the Academy of American Poets and Henri Coulette Memorial Poetry Award sponsored by California State University, Los Angeles, and was a finalist for the Howard Nemerov Sonnet Award sponsored by *The Formalist*.

She holds master's degrees in both Library Science and English Literature.

Visit her website at http://lidabushloper.com

www.ingramcontent.com/pod-product-compliance
Lightning Source LLC
Chambersburg PA
CBHW060332050426
42449CB00011B/2732